DOES CHRISTIANITY STILL MAKE SENSE?

SIX SESSIONS ON THE TOUGHEST OBJECTIONS TO CHRISTIANITY

STUDY GUIDE

Bobby Conway

TYNDALE
elevate™
ask. seek. find.

Visit Tyndale online at tyndale.com.

Tyndale and Tyndale's quill logo are registered trademarks of Tyndale House Ministries. Tyndale Elevate and the Tyndale Elevate logo are trademarks of Tyndale House Ministries. Tyndale Elevate is a nonfiction imprint of Tyndale House Publishers, Carol Stream, Illinois.

Does Christianity Still Make Sense? Study Guide: Six Sessions on the Toughest Objections to Christianity

Cover design by Libby Dykstra

Published in association with the literary agency of Mark Sweeney & Associates, Carol Stream, Illinois.

For information about special discounts for bulk purchases, please contact Tyndale House Publishers at csresponse@tyndale.com, or call 1-855-277-9400.

ISBN 978-1-4964-7647-0

Printed in the United States of America

30 29 28 27 26 25 24
7 6 5 4 3 2 1

DOES CHRISTIANITY STILL MAKE SENSE?

STUDY GUIDE

CONTENTS

INTRODUCTION

It has been several years now since God walked me out of an agonizing and extended season of doubt. To say those were some hard times would be an understatement. My anguishing dark night of the soul was marked by deep despair—the kind that can make you think about an exit strategy for life. To make matters worse, while I was feeling emotionally and spiritually flayed, I couldn't figure out how to resolve my doubts. My brain was producing questions faster than it could process them. My Christian walk began to feel like a long, drawn out Q&A session.

That's not good for anybody, and it certainly wasn't good for me. As I struggled along, one thing became increasingly clear: This side of heaven, I was never going to discover the airtight certainty I was looking for. Absolute assurance is beyond our reach. Nobody has all the answers in life—regardless of their belief system. Given the right circumstances, everyone is susceptible to a season of doubt. As hard as I pursued certainty, in the end it was a fool's errand.

What was I to do? Consumed with angst, I was struggling to make sense of Christianity. I was confused. Double-minded.

Intellectually twisted up. The solution had to be something other than discovering more answers—because there will always be more questions. What I needed, besides regaining the faith of a child, was to discover how to live with unanswered questions, while also rejoicing in the many answers I had already received through years of study. As I reflected on other worldviews, I came to see that each one had its own set of unanswered questions. After years of agonizing and thinking my way through various world religions, cults, secularism, and other life philosophies, I concluded that Christianity *still* makes sense. Pound for pound, it makes the best sense of all the options.

Remember when Jesus described himself as the Bread of Life?[1] That sermon marked a great departure for many of his would-be disciples. Jesus didn't make sense to them, so they left. But not all of them. Without adjusting his words to make them more palatable for his remaining followers, Jesus stuck to his message. Addressing the Twelve, he said, "Are you also going to leave?"[2] In other words, "Is *everyone* going to abandon me?"

In typical fashion, Simon Peter answered on behalf of the others: "Lord, to whom would we go? You have the words that give eternal life."[3] I love that. Peter was saying, "I'm not sure where those other folks are headed, but *we're* sticking with *you*, Jesus." Similarly, after I thought my way through various other belief options, I discovered there was nowhere else for me to go but home. So I did. In childlike faith, I surrendered my ignorance to God and trusted in his wisdom. And Christianity finally made sense again.

Perhaps you can relate. You're torn up with doubt. You find your faith wavering. Could you use some extra hope? Though this series aims to respond to some of the toughest objections to

Christianity, my purpose is bigger than simply finding answers to a bunch of questions. As important as it is to do our homework, making sense of Christianity ultimately comes by seeking the heart of God. If you are utterly lost in a maze of doubt, you need to know God more than you need the answer to another question.

As Christians, we have solid evidence to validate our trust in God. Our faith is not a shot in the dark. There is a wealth of compelling evidence in favor of Christianity that's worth unpacking. There are solid answers to life's toughest questions, and over the next six weeks we're going to make some sense of these together. As we turn our attention to the journey ahead, here's some guidance to get you started.

With only six weeks of discussions, we can barely scratch the surface of Christian apologetics. However, my hope is to whet your appetite for more.

Here's how the flow will go:

Each week, you'll start by watching, and discussing, a brief video that corresponds to a section in *Does Christianity Still Make Sense?*

Next, you will *read* a section composed of Bible verses and other information related to the topic of the session, and you will *respond* to several discussion questions.

The next section is designed to help you *prepare to act* on what you sense God is leading you to do in response.

Finally, the session will conclude with a time to *pray* together, inviting God to work through your group.

SESSION 1

WHEN CHRISTIANITY DIDN'T MAKE SENSE

BOBBY'S STORY OF NEARLY FALLING AWAY

There was . . . a castle called Doubting Castle,
the owner whereof was Giant Despair.
JOHN BUNYAN, *THE PILGRIM'S PROGRESS*

Before you meet for session 1,
read the introduction and chapters 1–4 in
Does Christianity Still Make Sense?

Does Christianity still make sense? This question haunts many Christians during seasons of doubt, when it seems as if their entire belief structure is being systematically dismantled. That was certainly my story. And the doubts were all the worse because I was the pastor of a large, thriving church and had developed a national reputation as a Christian apologist through my YouTube videos as the *One Minute Apologist* (now called *Christianity Still Makes Sense*). Yet there I was, a pastor, an author, and, yes, a Christian apologist, wondering whether Christianity still made sense. Had I been duped? For that agonizing season, it certainly felt that way.

Perhaps you can relate. Maybe you find yourself questioning a faith that once made sense to you. If so, be encouraged. There is a way forward. The purpose of this session is for us to get real with one another. The church should be a safe space. A place for believers to be able to doubt out loud in order to find a way to doubt toward faith once again. In Jude's epistle we read, "You must show mercy to those whose faith is wavering."[1] Let's aim to show that kind of mercy to anyone among us who is doubting.

Video

Before you open up your group time for discussion, watch the video for session 1.

Discuss

1. What stands out to you in Bobby's story? If it's something you relate to personally, share it with the group if you feel comfortable.

2. Have you ever gone through a significant season of doubt in your life? If so, how did you recover from that difficult time?

3. Why do you think it is often hard for Christians to talk about their doubts?

Read and Respond

The Bible is replete with stories about doubters—starting with Adam and Eve and continuing through Sarah and Abraham, Gideon, various prophets and psalmists, and on into the New Testament, including John the Baptist and some of Jesus' closest followers.

Here is a sampling of some folks in Scripture who grappled with their doubts. As you read the following passages, try to identify the various causes of doubt.

> John the Baptist, who was in prison, heard about all the things the Messiah was doing. So he sent his disciples to ask Jesus, "Are you the Messiah we've been expecting, or should we keep looking for someone else?"

Jesus told them, "Go back to John and tell him what you have heard and seen—the blind see, the lame walk, those with leprosy are cured, the deaf hear, the dead are raised to life, and the Good News is being preached to the poor." And he added, "God blesses those who do not fall away because of me."

As John's disciples were leaving, Jesus began talking about him to the crowds. "What kind of man did you go into the wilderness to see? Was he a weak reed, swayed by every breath of wind? Or were you expecting to see a man dressed in expensive clothes? No, people with expensive clothes live in palaces. Were you looking for a prophet? Yes, and he is more than a prophet. John is the man to whom the Scriptures refer when they say,

> 'Look, I am sending my messenger ahead of you,
> and he will prepare your way before you.'

"I tell you the truth, of all who have ever lived, none is greater than John the Baptist."[2]

1. How did someone like John the Baptist end up going through a season of doubt?

2. What does it tell you that he shared his doubts with his disciples?

3. In the final line of this excerpt, Jesus pays John quite the compliment, in spite of his doubt. What does that tell you about how Jesus regards our doubts?

One of the twelve disciples, Thomas (nicknamed the Twin), was not with the others when Jesus came. They told him, "We have seen the Lord!"

But he replied, "I won't believe it unless I see the nail wounds in his hands, put my fingers into them, and place my hand into the wound in his side."

Eight days later the disciples were together again, and this time Thomas was with them. The doors were locked; but suddenly, as before, Jesus was standing among them. "Peace be with you," he said. Then he said to Thomas, "Put your finger here, and look at my hands. Put your hand into the wound in my side. Don't be faithless any longer. Believe!"

"My Lord and my God!" Thomas exclaimed.

Then Jesus told him, "You believe because you have seen me. Blessed are those who believe without seeing me."[3]

4. It wasn't enough for Thomas to hear the eyewitness testimony of his fellow disciples. He wanted to see proof of Christ's resurrection for himself. Why do you think Thomas struggled to believe what he had heard?

5. Have you ever found yourself thinking like Thomas: *It'd be a whole lot easier to believe if I could just see*? Can you think of any examples in the Bible where seeing didn't necessarily equate to believing?

6. Sadly, Thomas became branded as "Doubting Thomas." What can Christians do to avoid labeling people based on something those people have said or done? How *should* we respond to people who express their doubts?

So they brought the boy. But when the evil spirit saw Jesus, it threw the child into a violent convulsion, and he fell to the ground, writhing and foaming at the mouth.

"How long has this been happening?" Jesus asked the boy's father.

He replied, "Since he was a little boy. The spirit often throws him into the fire or into water, trying to kill him. Have mercy on us and help us, if you can."

"What do you mean, 'If I can'?" Jesus asked. "Anything is possible if a person believes."

The father instantly cried out, "I do believe, but help me overcome my unbelief!"[4]

7. The father seems to have lost all hope because his child had suffered this way since he was a little boy. What is it about prolonged trials that can strip away our hope and faith?

8. What do you think the father meant when he said, "I do believe, but help me overcome my unbelief!"? How can faith and unbelief exist together?

9. The father received what he asked for. Have you ever prayed and felt ignored? How do you not lose heart when God remains silent or your prayers are not answered in the way that you want?

Prepare to Act

1. What are some of the biggest doubts that people struggle with in our culture today?

2. How do you think the church handles people's doubts overall? Is the church partly to blame for the doubts people are struggling with today? Why or why not?

3. What can the church do to better equip believers to navigate their way through their own doubts and the doubts expressed by others?

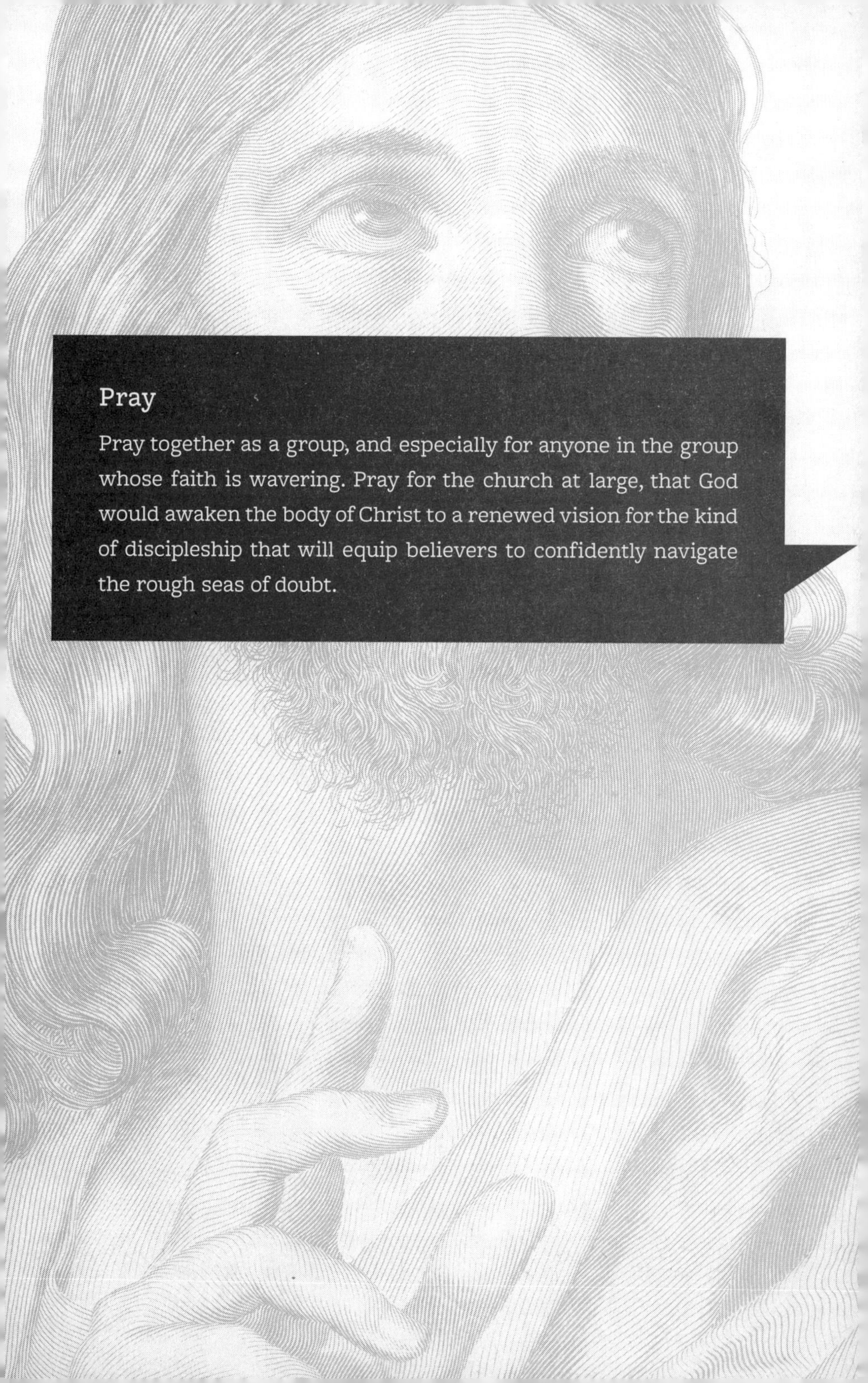

Pray

Pray together as a group, and especially for anyone in the group whose faith is wavering. Pray for the church at large, that God would awaken the body of Christ to a renewed vision for the kind of discipleship that will equip believers to confidently navigate the rough seas of doubt.

SESSION 2

WHAT'S WRONG WITH THE CHURCH?

SCANDALS, SCHISMS, AND SO MUCH MORE!

If you say that the history of the Church is a long succession of scandals, you are telling the truth, though if that is all you say, you are distorting the truth.

GERALD VANN

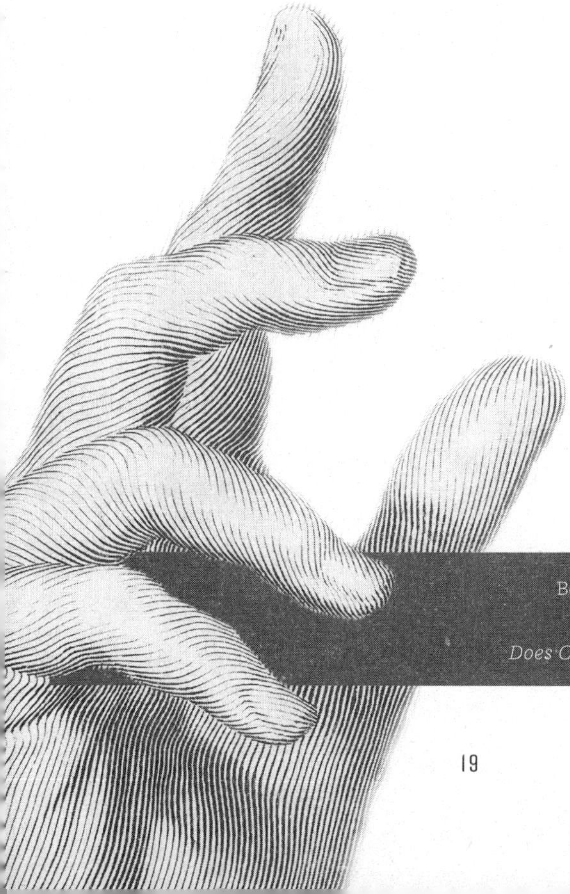

Before you meet for session 2, read chapters 5–13 in *Does Christianity Still Make Sense?*

It's no secret that the church has seen better days. You don't have to look far to find doctrinal compromise or disagreement within a denomination, a leader's moral or ethical failure, or stories of people who are leaving the church or even leaving the faith altogether. Every time we hear of another crisis in the church, it is tempting to ask, "What is wrong with the body of Christ?" The truth is that the church has had times of discord from the very beginning (see Acts 6:1-7). Several of the apostle Paul's letters were written to address conflict and scandal among believers. Just open your Bible to 1 Corinthians 1:10-12 or 5:1-12 and read for yourself. That church was a mess! And yet Paul still had high hopes for that quarrelsome, immoral group of believers.

The question I'm frequently asked is, "What's wrong with the church?"

Well, imperfect *people*, for one. People like you and me.

But this question needs a little more unpacking. So, let's talk about it.

Video

Before you open up your group time for discussion, watch the video for session 2.

Discuss

1. What stood out to you in today's video?

2. How would you describe the church's overall reputation?

3. Have you ever been challenged for sending mixed messages to those around you about your walk with Christ? If so, how did you respond?

Read and Respond

Not everyone who calls out to me, "Lord! Lord!" will enter the Kingdom of Heaven. Only those who actually do the will of my Father in heaven will enter. On judgment day many will say to me, "Lord! Lord! We prophesied in your name and cast out demons in your name and performed many miracles in your name." But I will reply, "I never knew you. Get away from me, you who break God's laws."[1]

1. What does it mean to do something "in Jesus' name"? What do these verses tell you about what Jesus thinks of hypocrisy?

2. How can these verses encourage someone who has become disillusioned with corrupted leaders in the church?

3. Does the existence of hypocrisy in the church discredit the truth of Christianity? Why or why not?

> Do not listen to an accusation against an elder unless it is confirmed by two or three witnesses.
>
> **1 TIMOTHY 5:19**

4. Why do you think the apostle Paul said that we should give the benefit of the doubt to Christian leaders unless there is more than one person who can back up an accusation against them? How have you seen this principle work, or not work, in the church?

5. What can churches do to safeguard against scandals, schisms, and abuses of power?

If another believer sins against you, go privately and point out the offense. If the other person listens and confesses it, you have won that person back. But if you are unsuccessful, take one or two others with you and go back again, so that everything you say may be confirmed by two or three witnesses. If the person still refuses to listen, take your case to the church. Then if he or she won't accept the church's decision, treat that person as a pagan or a corrupt tax collector.[2]

6. These verses are often referred to as a model for church discipline. Personally, I like the phrase *church restoration* a lot better. Who likes the idea of being disciplined? How much better to lovingly *restore* someone after a moral failure. Putting the emphasis on restoration creates a culture in which people will feel more safe and less shamed in the event they are confronted for their sin. Have you ever been a part of a church where the Matthew 18 process was used? If so, how was it handled? How did it work out?

> There is no longer Jew or Gentile, slave or free, male and female. For you are all one in Christ Jesus. And now that you belong to Christ, you are the true children of Abraham. You are his heirs, and God's promise to Abraham belongs to you.[3]

7. There has been a lot of talk lately about how oppressive the church is. Do you agree with that assessment? Why or why not? If so, why do you think that is?

8. What does Paul mean when he says that we are Abraham's children and heirs to his promise? How does this relate to the problem of believers oppressing one another in the church?

9. What are some ways the church has been used throughout history to liberate people who were living under oppression?

Prepare to Act

1. In what areas do you need to become more informed and learn how to address critiques of the church, so that you can offer a balanced reply about the many positive changes the church has brought about?

2. Set aside thirty to sixty minutes this week to reflect on the following questions: Where has your own example been less than ideal in the church, and what are you willing to do about it? What lies have you believed about the church that the culture has promoted? Where have you been naive about the church's failures? Have you minimized any moral failures around you or within you? Is there a moral issue you need to address in your own life or in the life of a Christian friend? Are you willing to lovingly act on this? Write down your observations and spend some time praying and confessing to the Lord where needed.

Pray

First John 1:9 says, "If we confess our sins to him, he is faithful and just to forgive us our sins and to cleanse us from all wickedness." Together as a group—first in silent confession and then praying aloud together—ask God to forgive you and the church at large and to help the church become the example he created us to be for the world.

SESSION 3

WHAT'S WRONG WITH GOD?

IF GOD IS GOOD, WHY IS THE WORLD SO JACKED UP?

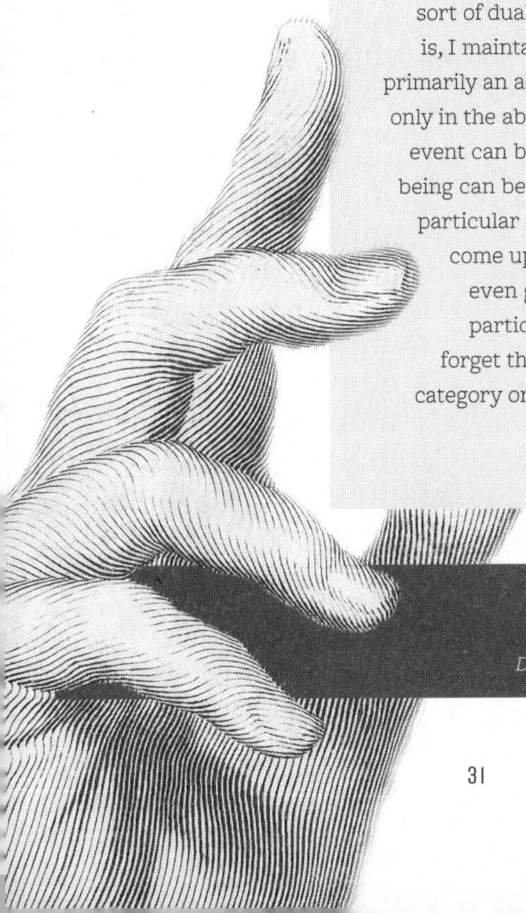

Evil is not a *something* that God could *create*. It isn't a kind of molecule or virus or forcefield or giant black nebula that courses through the universe, infecting or affecting everything it encounters. There was no time when God said, "Let there be evil," and there was evil. Nor has evil been eternally existent as some sort of dualistic counterpart to God. There is, I maintain, no such thing as evil. Evil is primarily an adjective, and it becomes a noun only in the abstract. An action can be evil, an event can be evil, a quality can be evil, or a being can be evil. And we can lump all these particular evils together in our minds and come up with the category *evil*. We can even go on to discuss it *as if it were* a particular thing, so long as we do not forget that we are always dealing with a category or group of particular evil things, not a thing itself.

JOHN G. STACKHOUSE JR.

Before you meet for session 3, read chapters 14–16 in *Does Christianity Still Make Sense?*

Evil is a universally recognized phenomenon, but there isn't a universal explanation for it. Differing worldviews offer different explanations to questions such as, "What is evil?" "Where did evil come from?" and, "If God exists, why does he allow evil to permeate our world?" These questions are always relevant, and the answers vary depending on one's worldview. Let's consider a few of these explanations here.

First, let's look at atheism. An atheist might argue as follows:

1. If there were a God, and God were all-powerful, he could destroy evil.
2. If there were a God, and God were all-good, he would destroy evil.
3. Evil is not destroyed.
4. Therefore, God does not exist, or God is not all-good and all-powerful.

Or consider pantheism, which posits that all is God. A pantheist might say something like this:

1. God is all there is, and all is God.
2. God is good.
3. Therefore, evil cannot exist.
4. Otherwise, God (and humans, for that matter, because we are all collectively God) would be evil.

In other words, the pantheist would explain away evil as an illusion.

Next consider polytheism, the belief in many gods. A polytheist might argue accordingly:

1. There is such a thing as evil.
2. There are many gods at war against evil.
3. Hopefully, one day good will win out against evil.

This was the way the ancient Greeks believed. They were polytheistic and believed the gods were engaged in a cosmic battle. There are certainly more options to consider, but due to space, let's now think about how a Christian would account for evil:

1. If God is all-powerful, he can destroy evil.
2. If God is all-good, he will destroy evil.
3. Since God is all-powerful and all-good, he can, and he will, destroy evil.

God's power and goodness are not compromised. But it's a matter of *timing*. It isn't that God isn't just, or that he is sitting on his hands; but his timing for intervention doesn't necessarily run according to our timetable. Even things that appear to be unaddressed will ultimately be addressed in the end, when at last God will destroy evil and everyone will be held justly accountable for the life they lived.

Video

Before you open up your group time for discussion, watch the video for session 3.

Discuss

1. What stood out to you in today's video?

2. How would you reply to someone who says they can't believe in a God who would allow the world to contain so much evil?

3. Reread the John G. Stackhouse Jr. quote at the beginning of this session. How does it affect your understanding of evil to see it as a descriptive adjective rather than a concrete noun?

Read and Respond

> Give thanks to the LORD, for he is good!
> His faithful love endures forever.[1]

> This is the message we heard from Jesus and now declare to you: God is light, and there is no darkness in him at all.[2]

> Then God looked over all he had made, and he saw that it was very good![3]

1. What do these verses teach us about God and creation?

2. Why do people want to blame God for all the evil in the world?

3. There are two types of evils—*natural evils* that result from things such as hurricanes, earthquakes, tornadoes, etc.; and *moral evils* that result from our free will. How can focusing on God's goodness in the face of evil outcomes help us?

As for you, you meant evil against me, but God meant it for good, to bring it about that many people should be kept alive, as they are today.[4]

4. This verse refers to Joseph's moment of reconciliation with his brothers after they sold him into slavery. Here we can see his perspective. What does it tell you about Joseph that he could respond in this way?

5. Have you ever suffered an injustice where you adopted a similar perspective?

6. What might have happened if Joseph didn't have this perspective? And how would the betrayal that he had experienced continue to affect his life?

Prepare to Act

Even though the fig trees have no blossoms,
    and there are no grapes on the vines;
even though the olive crop fails,
    and the fields lie empty and barren;
even though the flocks die in the fields,
    and the cattle barns are empty,
yet I will rejoice in the LORD!
    I will be joyful in the God of my salvation![5]

1. The book of Habakkuk tells the story of how a doubting prophet shifted his perspective as he came to trust in God's goodness, even though he couldn't understand many of God's ways. Why is it important not to question God's goodness when evil comes our way?

2. Habakkuk was aware that he could lose everything, and yet he was determined to rejoice in the Lord. In a life full of evils, how can deciding in advance to not be sour toward God help us through the tough times we encounter?

3. What spiritual resources has God given us so that we will not lose hope?

Pray

Pray together as a group about some current events where evil seems to be prevailing. Ask God to help your local church and the church at large to serve as powerful lights in our dark world.

SESSION 4

WHY IS CHRISTIANITY SO EXCLUSIVE?

THOSE NARROW-MINDED CHRISTIANS

Our awareness of "religious others" has never been more acute than it is today, forcing the church to deal with new and troubling questions that pose formidable challenges to traditional Christian beliefs and practices.

HAROLD NETLAND

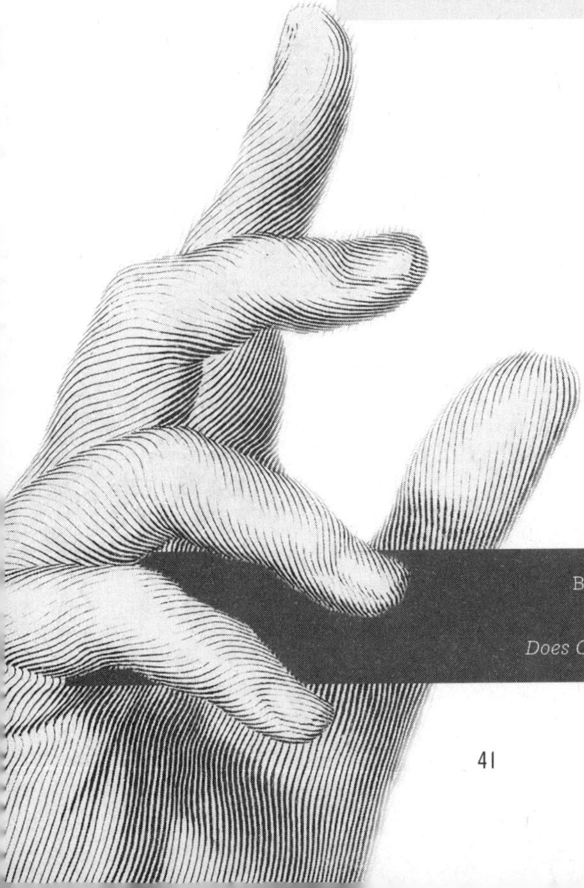

Before you meet for session 4, read chapters 17–20 in *Does Christianity Still Make Sense?*

Over the years, I've had many conversational encounters with non-Christians. Typically, it doesn't take long before I hear the objection that Christianity is "too exclusive." I've heard many people say that getting to heaven is like climbing a mountain. "There's not just one way; lots of paths will get you there." Though that may be true for mountaineering, it isn't the case for getting to heaven. If there were another way for us to get to heaven, don't you think Jesus would've chosen it? I mean, why go through what he did if there were another way?

The idea that there are several paths leading to our eternal destination is rooted in religious pluralism, which isn't foreign to our culture. In fact, one of the reasons God's people went into captivity was because they sought to adopt the gods of the surrounding nations. God wasn't a fan of religious pluralism then, nor is he now. Religious pluralists can be detected through statements such as these:

"It doesn't matter what you believe, as long as you're sincere."
"As long as it works for you and makes you happy, that's what counts."
"There is no such thing as ultimate (or absolute) truth."
"There are many ways to God."
"It's rude to say one person's religion is better than another's."
"It takes everyone's truth to equal the truth."
"What makes you think your religion is right and everyone else's is wrong?"
"Only narrow-minded people believe that Jesus is the only way to heaven."
"It would be unfair for there to only be one way to heaven."

Do any of these statements sound familiar? I trust they do. That's because sentiments like these express the mindset of many in our culture today. Religious pluralists are more than ready to raise their objections against Christianity. The real question is whether we are ready to furnish them with answers.

Video

Before you open up your group time for discussion, watch the video for session 4.

Discuss

1. What stood out to you in today's video?

2. In your opinion, what has influenced the rise of religious pluralism in our culture today?

3. Why do you think religious pluralism is so attractive to so many people?

Read and Respond

Jesus told him, "I am the way, the truth, and the life. No one can come to the Father except through me."[1]

1. How do you think a religious pluralist would interpret this verse (John 14:6)?

There is salvation in no one else! God has given no other name under heaven by which we must be saved.[2]

2. The apostle Peter, speaking to the Sanhedrin (the council of rulers, elders, and teachers of religious law in Jerusalem), affirmed the truth that Jesus is the only way to heaven. Why is that significant? Why do you think that some people continue to insist there must be another way?

Everyone who acknowledges me publicly here on earth, I will also acknowledge before my Father in heaven. But everyone who denies me here on earth, I will also deny before my Father in heaven.[3]

3. Now that we've been on this journey together for several weeks, let's do a gut check. Do you recognize Jesus as your exclusive Lord and Savior? If not, what obstacles remain that may be preventing you from trusting Christ? Share your answer with the group if you feel comfortable.

4. One valid concern that many people have is the fate of those who've never heard about Jesus. Discuss the possibility that God would judge them according to the light they've been given—in other words, could they be saved because of what Jesus did for them on the cross, even though they may not have heard that specific information yet?

Prepare to Act

1. This week, write down all the objections you can think of that religious pluralists might make against Jesus being the only way to heaven. Then think through and jot down biblical responses you might offer in reply. Get together with someone from your group this week to exchange thoughts.

2. Have you ever known anyone who was "spiritual but not religious"? What were their beliefs and behaviors? How might you encourage someone in that position to again consider attending church?

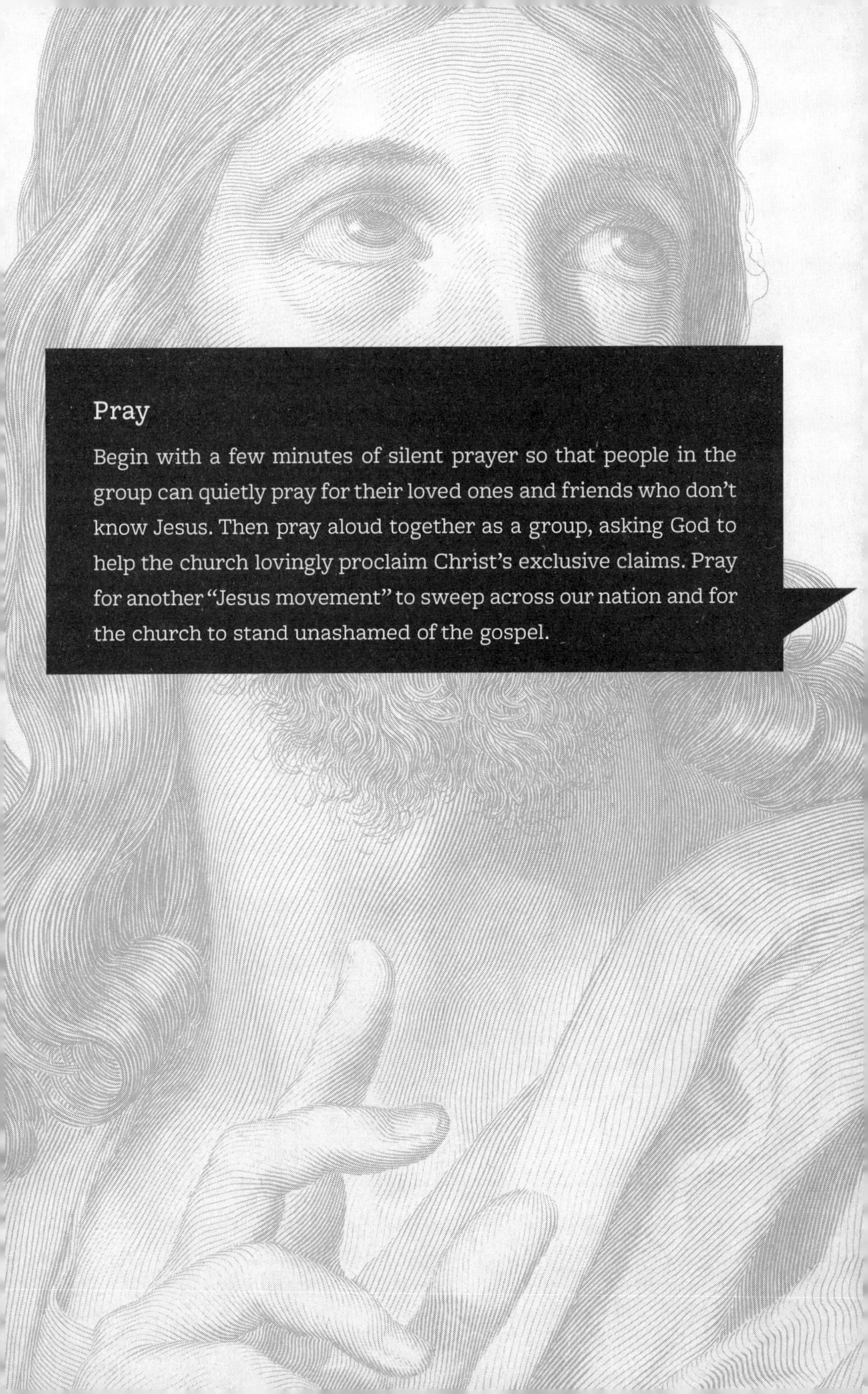

Pray

Begin with a few minutes of silent prayer so that people in the group can quietly pray for their loved ones and friends who don't know Jesus. Then pray aloud together as a group, asking God to help the church lovingly proclaim Christ's exclusive claims. Pray for another "Jesus movement" to sweep across our nation and for the church to stand unashamed of the gospel.

SESSION 5

HASN'T SCIENCE BURIED GOD?

CHRISTIANITY AND ITS COMPATIBILITY WITH SCIENCE

> This most beautiful system of the sun, planets, and comets could only proceed from the counsel and dominion of an intelligent and powerful being.
>
> ***ISAAC NEWTON***

> The more I study nature, the more I stand amazed at the work of the Creator. Science brings men nearer to God.
>
> ***LOUIS PASTEUR***

Before you meet for session 5, read chapters 21–25 in *Does Christianity Still Make Sense?*

Ever since the Age of Enlightenment, there has been no shortage of atheists contending that God is an unnecessary hypothesis. Some have even gone so far as to ridicule anyone who still believes in God. But even though science has made great advances in the world, has it buried the need for God? Is God a mere relic of the past, a useful fiction that served its purpose and is now ready to be swept into the dustbin of history? Not quite.

The belief that science is sufficient to answer everything we need to know, also called scientism, comes with its own inherent problems—beginning with methodological naturalism, the method by which science is done. By presupposing that the material world is all that exists, scientism seeks to preclude a theological perspective from the outset. Though naturalism may be a convenient theory for ardent materialists to build on, it fails to do justice to the wider spectrum of inquiry that opens up when room for God is allowed in our search for answers.

In this session, we'll see that science hasn't buried God, but neither has God buried the purpose of investigating our universe scientifically. Many scientists may be anti-God, but God is not anti-science. What God is against is scientists ignoring that he's the one who put the universe there in the first place.

Video

Before you open up your group time for discussion, watch the video for session 5.

Discuss

1. What stood out to you in today's video?

2. Why do you think some people are so eager to try to exclude God from our understanding of science and the universe?

3. Have you ever heard that God and science are at odds with one another? How do you respond to that line of thinking? How does it influence you?

4. Have you ever had a conversation with an atheist about your respective beliefs? How did the interaction go? What were his or her biggest objections to Christianity?

5. It's not unusual for atheists to present themselves as having a superior intellectual worldview—using statements such as, "I just follow the science," or "Religion is a crutch for weak-minded people." How can we as Christians respond to statements such as these?

Read and Respond

Herbert Spencer, the nineteenth-century polymath who coined the phrase "survival of the fittest," also claimed that all of existence could be explained by one of five categories: *time*, *force*, *action*, *space*, and *matter*. Though Spencer's thesis was widely celebrated by his scientific peers, it turns out God was way ahead of him, as can be seen in the very first verse of the Bible: "In the beginning God created the heavens and the earth."[1]

Here's how Spencer's hypothesis lines up with Scripture: "In the beginning [time] God [force] created [action] the heavens [space] and the earth [matter]." It's as if God anticipated objections to his existence from the get-go.

1. What encourages you about connecting Spencer's five categories to Scripture?

2. What are the dangers of trying to impose scientific findings on the Bible? What is the danger of ignoring science altogether?

3. Do you think the church is adequately equipping our young people to think for themselves? How can college students defend their faith when atheist professors try to convince them that science has buried the need for God? What are some steps the church can take to help the emerging generation develop a stronger biblical foundation?

The heavens proclaim the glory of God.
    The skies display his craftsmanship.
Day after day they continue to speak;
    night after night they make him known.
They speak without a sound or word;
    their voice is never heard.
Yet their message has gone throughout the earth,
    and their words to all the world.
God has made a home in the heavens for the sun.[2]

> God shows his anger from heaven against all sinful, wicked people who suppress the truth by their wickedness. They know the truth about God because he has made it obvious to them. For ever since the world was created, people have seen the earth and sky. Through everything God made, they can clearly see his invisible qualities—his eternal power and divine nature. So they have no excuse for not knowing God.[3]

4. The above verses refer to God's general revelation as depicted in nature. Taking both passages together, what stands out to you the most?

5. How have some of the scientific discoveries in the modern era reinforced the message of these two passages? To get your thoughts turning, think about discoveries made through inventions such as the Hubble Space Telescope and how they have bolstered the claims of these verses. If the psalmist was blown away by God's glory in creation without a telescope, how much more should we be blown away by these further discoveries?

Even Gentiles, who do not have God's written law, show that they know his law when they instinctively obey it, even without having heard it. They demonstrate that God's law is written in their hearts, for their own conscience and thoughts either accuse them or tell them they are doing right. And this is the message I proclaim—that the day is coming when God, through Christ Jesus, will judge everyone's secret life.[4]

6. These verses relate to God's general revelation as etched on our consciences. What stands out to you in these verses? How do you think an atheist would explain the existence of conscience?

7. When we experience a disruption in our conscience and we feel guilty, why does it feel *personal*—like we're being watched?

8. Guilt is like a check engine light. Why do you think many people today are willing to ignore guilt? Or what are some strategies people use to cope with their guilt?

> Only fools say in their hearts,
> "There is no God."[5]

9. Why do you think the Bible refers to people who say there is no God as fools?

10. Do you think there is less evidence of God's existence today or more? Explain.

11. Do you think *more evidence* is what atheists need the most? Why or why not?

Prepare to Act

1. As Christians, we must be prepared to interact with people who don't share our beliefs. This includes atheists who are ready to contend that science has rendered God irrelevant. Where do you need to strengthen yourself to be ready for these discussions? What are some immediate steps you can take to become better equipped?

2. Subscribe to the *Unbelievable* podcast (https://unbelievable.podbean.com). Though Justin Brierley no longer hosts the show, he moderated conversations between Christians and atheists for more than ten years, and there is a wealth of information to be learned from these discussions. This podcast is a great way to equip yourself on the issues that Christians face, and a helpful way to learn how to converse in a Christian way with atheists.

Pray

Pray together as a group, asking God to help everyone in your group find opportunities to become more equipped to discuss the interface between faith and science.

SESSION 6

WHERE DO WE GO FROM HERE?

A CALL FOR A NEW REFORMATION

Every age has had its darkness and its dangers. The task of the Christian is not to whine about the moment in which he or she lives but to understand its problems and respond appropriately to them.

CARL R. TRUEMAN

Reformation is a return to the sound doctrine of the Bible. Revival is the practice of that sound doctrine under the power of the Holy Spirit.

FRANCIS SCHAEFFER

Before you meet for session 6, read the conclusion and afterword in *Does Christianity Still Make Sense?*

On October 31, 1517, Martin Luther nailed his Ninety-Five Theses to the door of the Castle Church in Wittenberg, Germany. These contentions codified his arguments against the Catholic Church of his day. With one bold move, Luther lit the match that sparked the beginning of the Protestant Reformation. Having taken a few Reformation tours, and having stood at the door of the Castle Church, I can say that if there was ever a time for a new reformation, that time is now. The church in America is in shambles. In today's session, let's consider the way forward as we try to discern what it will take to bring about such a reformation.

Video

Before you open up your group time for discussion, watch the video for session 6.

Discuss

1. What stood out to you in today's video?

2. Do you agree that the church needs some sort of reformation today? Why or why not?

3. If God were to call on you to become a modern-day Luther to today's church, what would the main points of your theses be?

4. Do you think another Reformation is possible? What positive and negative lessons can we learn from the Protestant Reformation in the sixteenth century?

5. What will a new reformation require of us? What potential consequences must we be prepared for?

Read and Respond

As Martin Luther said when appearing before the Diet of Worms to give an account for his Ninety-Five Theses, "Unless I am convicted by Scripture and plain reason (I do not accept the authority of popes and councils because they have contradicted each other), my conscience is captive to the Word of God. I cannot and will not recant anything, for to go against conscience is neither right nor safe. So help me God. Amen."[1]

1. Luther was asked to recant what he had written. Under threat of excommunication, he wasn't willing to yield. Instead he said, "My conscience is captive to the Word of God." What a statement. Where do you feel we are being challenged to compromise our conscience today?

2. Why do you think so many Christians today lack Luther's strong conviction? What would it take for you to develop an uncompromising conviction to stand on the authority of God's Word?

Hezekiah was twenty-five years old when he became the king of Judah, and he reigned in Jerusalem twenty-nine years. His mother was Abijah, the daughter of Zechariah. He did what was pleasing in the LORD's sight, just as his ancestor David had done.

In the very first month of the first year of his reign, Hezekiah reopened the doors of the Temple of the LORD and repaired them. He summoned the priests and Levites to meet him at the courtyard east of the Temple. He said to them, "Listen to me, you Levites! Purify yourselves, and purify the Temple of the LORD, the God of your ancestors. Remove all the defiled things from the sanctuary. Our ancestors were unfaithful and did what was evil in the sight of the LORD our God. They abandoned the LORD and his dwelling place; they turned their backs on him. They also shut the doors to the Temple's entry room, and they snuffed out the lamps. They stopped burning incense and presenting burnt offerings at the sanctuary of the God of Israel.

"That is why the LORD's anger has fallen upon Judah and Jerusalem. He has made them an object of dread, horror, and ridicule, as you can see with your own eyes. Because of this, our fathers have been killed in battle, and our sons and daughters and wives have been captured. But now I will make a covenant with the LORD, the God of Israel, so that his fierce anger will turn away from us. My sons, do not neglect your duties any longer! The LORD has chosen you to stand in his presence, to minister to him, and to lead the people in worship and present offerings to him."[2]

3. Hezekiah was one of the kings who brought about positive reform among God's people. Who are some other reformers in the Bible you can think of? Who are some other reformers throughout church history?

4. Why did God's people need reform under Hezekiah's kingship?

5. What were some of the consequences God's people encountered because they turned away from the Lord?

6. Do you think there are still consequences today for turning away from God? What does that look like? What can we learn from Hezekiah's leadership as it relates to seeing reformation in our own day? What character qualities should we look for in people with the leadership capacity to lead us toward reform?

For a time is coming when people will no longer listen to sound and wholesome teaching. They will follow their own desires and will look for teachers who will tell them whatever their itching ears want to hear. They will reject the truth and chase after myths.

But you should keep a clear mind in every situation. Don't be afraid of suffering for the Lord. Work at telling others the Good News, and fully carry out the ministry God has given you.[3]

7. What are your thoughts on this message from Paul to his protégé Timothy? Do you think that *time* he refers to has come to us in America?

8. What are some false teachings that have crept into the church today that must be eradicated?

Prepare to Act

1. In the last chapter of *Does Christianity Still Make Sense?*, I share four actions steps I believe the church must take to move toward reformation:

   - Identify the problems in the church that need reforming.
   - Encourage bold and wise leaders to find ways to unify the church at large.
   - Break the silence and start using our voices as agents of change.
   - Recognize that reformation comes at a cost.

With these four thoughts in mind, set aside some time this week to make a list of areas where you think the church needs reformation.

2. Ask God to show you how he wants to use *you* to help bring about reform within the church. Use the space below to jot some notes. Think about the influencers you know and invite them to network with you and other churches. Join together to pray for vision and a plan to see God bring it about. Don't expect this to be easy. There's a lot of work to be done, but by God's grace we will succeed.

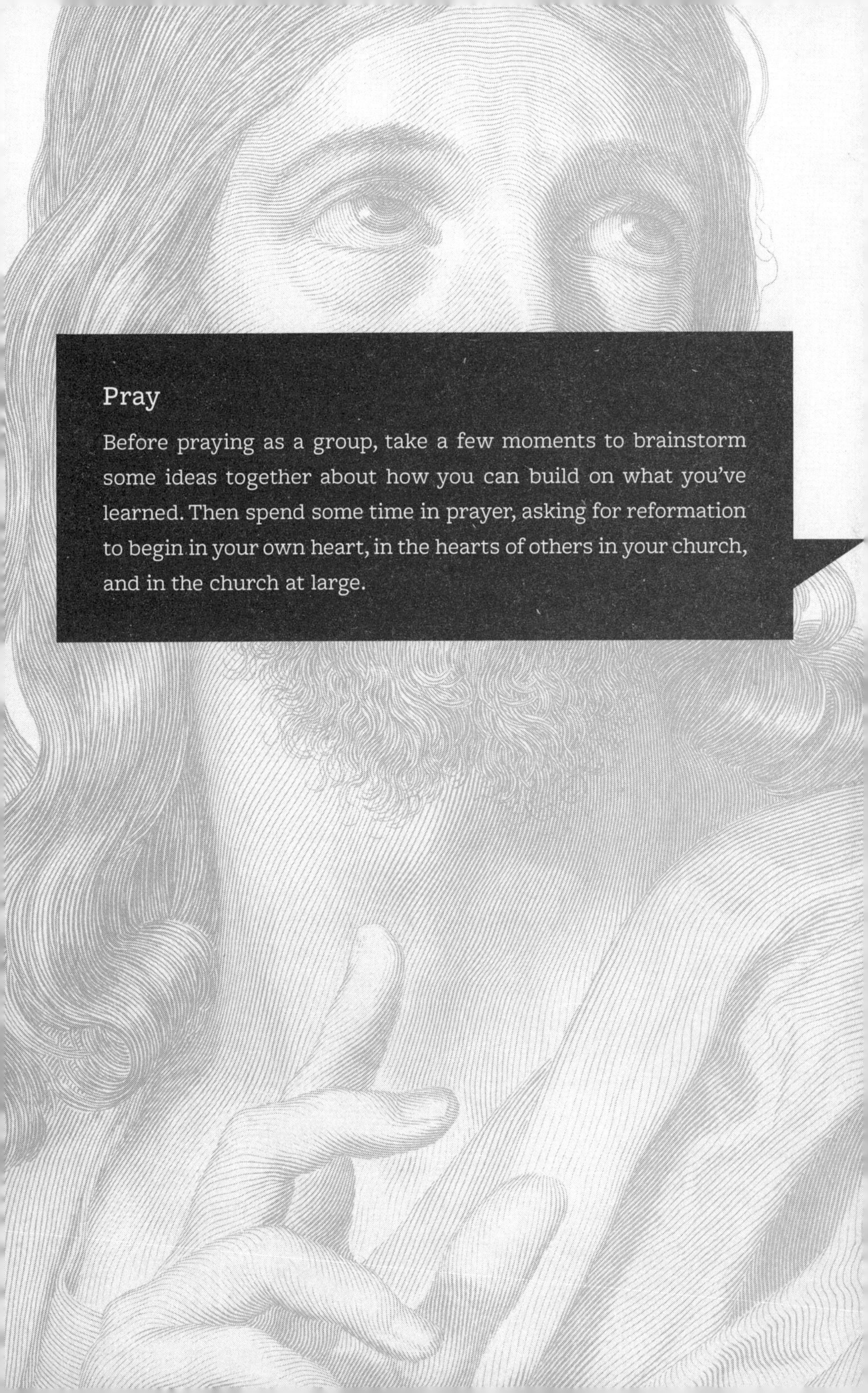

Pray

Before praying as a group, take a few moments to brainstorm some ideas together about how you can build on what you've learned. Then spend some time in prayer, asking for reformation to begin in your own heart, in the hearts of others in your church, and in the church at large.

NOTES

INTRODUCTION

1. John 6:22-58.
2. John 6:67.
3. John 6:68.

SESSION 1: WHEN CHRISTIANITY DIDN'T MAKE SENSE

1. Jude 1:22.
2. Matthew 11:2-11.
3. John 20:24-29.
4. Mark 9:20-24.

SESSION 2: WHAT'S WRONG WITH THE CHURCH?

1. Matthew 7:21-23.
2. Matthew 18:15-17.
3. Galatians 3:28-29.

SESSION 3: WHAT'S WRONG WITH GOD?

1. Psalm 118:29.
2. 1 John 1:5.
3. Genesis 1:31.
4. Genesis 50:20, ESV.
5. Habakkuk 3:17-18.

SESSION 4: WHY IS CHRISTIANITY SO EXCLUSIVE?

1. John 14:6.
2. Acts 4:12.
3. Matthew 10:32-33.

SESSION 5: HASN'T SCIENCE BURIED GOD?

1. Genesis 1:1.
2. Psalm 19:1-4.
3. Romans 1:18-20.
4. Romans 2:14-16.
5. Psalm 14:1.

SESSION 6: WHERE DO WE GO FROM HERE?

1. Martin Luther, quoted in Dan Graves, "Here I stand, I can do no other, so help me God. Amen," Christian History Institute (blog), https://christianhistoryinstitute.org/blog/post/here-i-stand-i-can-do-no-other.
2. 2 Chronicles 29:1-11.
3. 2 Timothy 4:3-5.

ABOUT THE AUTHOR

Bobby Conway serves as lead pastor of Image Church in Charlotte, North Carolina, and he is well known for his YouTube ministry, *Christianity Still Makes Sense* (formerly *One Minute Apologist*). He also serves as the cohost of *Pastors' Perspective*, a nationally syndicated radio show on KWVE in Southern California. Bobby is the author of several books, including *The Fifth Gospel* and *Doubting Toward Faith*. He holds a PhD in philosophy of religion from the University of Birmingham in England and resides in Charlotte with his wife, Heather. They have two adult children, Haley and Dawson.